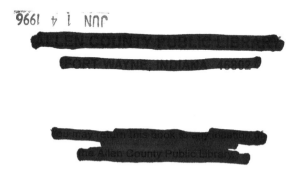

JOKES
TO TELL YOUR
FRIENDS

Library of Congress Catalog-in-Publication Data
Woodworth, Viki
Jokes to Tell Your Friends / Viki Woodworth.
p. cm.
Summary: A collection of jokes that can be shared.
Example: On what side of the house do trees grow?
The outside!

ISBN 1-56766-099-1
1. Wit and humor, Juvenile [1. Jokes.]
I. Title.
PN6163.W6833 1995   93-7834
818'.5402–dc20   CIP/AC

JOKES
TO TELL YOUR
FRIENDS

Compiled and Illustrated by
Viki Woodworth

Char: What is that following your horse?
Erin: Its tail.

Stan: How long will the next bus be?
Brad: As long as all the rest!

Jess: I know a baby who drinks dog milk.
Tess: Really?
Jess? Yes, it's a baby dog.

Kai: I'm going to put something in this doughnut.
Letta: What?
Kai: My teeth.

Alex: You're squinting. Have your eyes ever been checked?
Maxine: No, they've always been green.

4

Ken: Are caterpillars tasty?
Brad: How would I know?
Ken: You just ate one in your salad.

Eileen: What is your chicken doing in the middle of the road?

Stuart: She wanted to lay one on the line.

1st Chicken: Why did you throw that egg at me?

2nd Chicken: Because the yolk's on you!

Don: I'm homesick.

Joe: You are home.

Don: Yup. I'm sick of it.

Joe: Why won't your dog go outside?

Al: Because it's a dog-eat-dog world out there!

Richard: What kind of animals live at the North Pole?

Crissie: Cold ones!

Stan: How will you fix that tuba?
Anne: With a tuba glue, of course!

Roger: My chicken can't find her eggs.
Shirley: Why not?
Roger: She mislaid them.

Jason: What does your dog eat at the movies?
Brad: Pupcorn.

Bruce: I swallowed a roll of film. What should I do?
Sarah: Just wait and see what develops.

Carole: I think this milk came from a pampered cow.
Patty: Why?
Carole: It's spoiled.

Peggy: What do I need to know to teach my dog tricks?
Rick: More than your dog!

Emily: I heard your dog was in love.
Brad: Yeah, but it's over now. It was only puppylove.

Shirley: Is your chicken telling jokes?
Roger: Yes, she's a comedi-hen.

Dan: Your dog has fleas, but he never scratches. Why?
Sid: He's so gentle he wouldn't even hurt a flea.

George: Our dog is just like one of the family.
Sandy: I know, I've seen your brother.

Christine: I think this milk came from a rabbit.
Eliza: Why?
Christine: I found a hare in it.

Sheila: I think it's raining cats and dogs.
Pete: Why?
Sheila: I just stepped in a poodle!

Jane: Why are you putting shortening in your hair?
Brian: To keep it from growing.

1st Witch: How's your new house?
2nd Witch: Awful. It doesn't even have a broom closet.

Kathy: I just saw a field of corn that was lying down.
Joyce: Why?
Kathy: It was pooped corn.

Ben: How long can a person live without a brain?
Ann: I don't know, how old are you?

Bill: Have you seen the English Channel?
Lil: No, we don't have cable T.V.

Mike: Do you know what has no beginning and no end?
Roy: No.
Mike: A circle.

**Steve: What does that two-headed
sheep say?**
Asa: I don't know.
Steve: Baa. Baa.

Joan: How did they invent macaroni?
Phil: Someone really used their noodle.

Terrie: Why did you tell everyone I was a creep?
Sasha: Sorry. I didn't know it was a secret.

Britteny: I have the loudest pet.
Claire: What kind is it?
Britteny: A trum-pet.

Chris: Why are you throwing that clock out the window?
Bruce: I want to see time fly.

Ashley: Why are these seats so clean?
Matt: They're bleachers.

Kim: Which reptile knows how to use the telephone?
Tim: I don't know.
Kim: The croco-dial.

Nan: How can I stop my nose from running?
Diane: Tape it to your face.

Laura: My dog is lost!
Nora: Put an ad in the paper.
Laura: But my dog can't read.

Brian: My teacher punished me for something I didn't do.
Eric: What?
Brian: My homework.

Max: Why did you put that mousetrap in the freezer?
Lem: To get a cold snap!

Jackie: Why are you putting wheels on your rocking chair?
Mack: So I can rock and roll.

Sandy: Watch out for that clock!
George: Why?
Sandy: It's ready to strike.

Marta: I heard you got a flat tire on your bike.

Ian: Yeah, there was a fork in the road.

Margaret: My dad hasn't worked a day in years.

Barb: Why not?

Margaret: He works at night.

Marsha: I like to sleep with my dog.

Sylvia: Why?

Marsha: He's an Afghan.

Tina: Where are you from?

Adam: Kansas.

Tina: What part?

Adam: All of me.

Ann: You'll have to pay when you go to school.

Ben: Pay what?

Ann: Pay attention!

Ed: What shall I do with my sick canary?
Ted: Take him in for tweetment.

Heidi: What is that owl reading?
Zack: A who-done-it.

Todd: My jacket is just plain lazy!
Charlie: Why do you say that?
Todd: It just hangs around all the time.

Pam: Do you know which poet is a great baseball player?
Sally: No, which one?
Pam: Homer, of course.

Allie: We have a new class at school where we write on maps.
Meg: Really, what's it called?
Allie: Geogra-fiti.

Diane: My dog is mad at me.
Nan: How can you tell?
Diane: He won't speak to me.

Miles: Why are you planting lightbulbs?
Charlotte: We need more light in our yard.

Brad: That clock must be hungry.
Jason: Why?
Brad: It's going back for seconds.

Peggy: My granddad raises horses.
Bill: Wow. He must be strong!

Girl Skeleton: Why are you going to the beach?
Boy Skeleton: To get a skele-tan.

Charlie: How'd you get your dog to stop barking?
Becky: We gave him a yappin-dectomy.

Jill: I'm going to make something you can't see!
Jack: What?
Jill: Noise!

Daniel: Our pig just said "moo"!
Bob: No kidding, why?
Daniel: She's learning a second language.